A LIGHT LEFT ON

RACHEL MANLEY

A LIGHT LEFT ON

PEEPAL TREE

First published in Britain in 1992
Peepal Tree Books
17 King's Avenue
Leeds LS6 1QS
Yorkshire
England

ISBN 0 948833 55 6

FOR MY FATHER

With special thanks to
Wayne Brown, Lorna Goodison
and my brother Joseph
for their help and enthusiasm

and to Uncle Douglas
with whom I share
the special bond of laughter

CONTENTS

THE GATE (FOR E.M)

Don't turn back at the garden gate;
it's late, the afternoon is tired
and waits to take you home.
No need to say goodbye,
parting is only
the marking of a book's page
to which you will return.
All of the years we shared
belong to us,
a story that we told
and cared about enough
to keep with us.
Yes, time will fall away,
moment by moment,
but the gate remains
shut, but not locked,
at the edge of memory.
Come back to see me
when you have the time;
bring this soft afternoon
and do not leave behind
a note of birds' song.
Let the gentle wind
unfold each page
from where you left.
Believe
that I could take no journey
further than
the landscape that we painted
with our lives.
Know, without sorrow,
that the edge of night,
the last line of the page,

only saves the day,
shelters the story.
Boundaries do not kill,
they just contain.
Tears you take into the night
will not flow back to me.
I am here, locked
in the laughter, in the life
of your remembrance;
don't turn back at the garden gate.

REGARDLESS

All of us,
bruised by our own
degree of caring,
sat at the edge
of your garden

sensed by the watchful
almond tree
a strong nanny
moved little by time

Around the house
the ginger lilies
pulled their oars
against the breeze
and the hills beyond
remained loyal.

Poinsettias still glow
like Christmas decorations
on a January tree

plumbago blooms
arrive each year
like guests
well-dressed for tea.

REGARDLESS II

Being here
at the nerve's edge
where thoughts bloom
like matins
through light.
I return
to this garden
where the birds
interrupt flight
and we are the congregation.

The limbs of the hills
stretch olympic across the sky
the wind is the will
who bends the elbows of trees
beats my soul into peace;

      I am here
at the nerve's edge
where old testaments
roll in like waves
and break.

THE ANCESTOR

You will chisel bone,
mallet-hard hand,
you will hatch me,

sculpt muscles belligerent and strong,
model me the ox: cast me in bronze;
weave me in anguished black,
unpatterned, without dreams:
so is my destiny.

Ancestor, mother-tall by years,
over my shoulder your light stares
at my sons: I am too near;
you are too strong, too sad,
and I, I am full of tears,
my songs choked by your battle cries.

ORPHEUS — "THE LISTENER"

Do fingers play,
old Orpheus,
or is it that they listen?
What is the music
that I feel in me,
and Euridice in you?
Is it the legend
from the throat of memory;
the journey of the notes
that rhyme upon the mind?
Are we mad ladies
poised like peacocks
at a poem's edge?
Was it a song
or notes fixed into stone
against the wash of time,
sound of the recurring wave,
the scent of pines,
that stay with us?

Night blooms
but the fingers listen
till they know the hurt
by heart.

PRAISE

I am Praise.
I rise like incense
from the soul's fire!
Let my youth be your beauty,
let my strength bear your journey.
I have made time bend
its limbs in the breeze,
my joy is the shape of your laughter
I have parted the wind.
My soul is the Lord's eye
and has led me to sin and truth.
Praise is the lightning of prayer,
the silhouette of thunder.

FORTY

By forty I had lost you.
Sleep had quietly shut the door,
just for a while, I thought,
as though you and Par were resting...
but this is different.
Now they honour you.
As I walk down the path
I remember a life full of stars
and a bright white moon
where we saw ladies dance,
and the solitaire sang so sadly
that the pines wept
and left poems on the ground....
we'd find them in the morning.
All the way down to the gate
I could hear your footsteps
tracing his, and all the way back
your footsteps alone, picking up courage.
Now I am forty and I think I will
dance right off the edge of the moon.

MEMORY

The afternoon belongs to my grandfather.
You cannot take it away
though the mind darkens
and the children's laughter
has strayed like messages.
I am near the verandah,
lost in my nets of thought
which I brought from age six,
a very long way.
You cannot sentence memory to death,
it returns through the years
lulled into hymns.
If I close my eyes
Time will forget me;
I hear an old lady reading from Rilke,
she finds the best line
and explains
that poets don't have to rhyme anymore.
If I close my eyes
my hands will forget me,
I'm up in the plum tree
near to the sky;
if I leave, I'll never come back.
Here in this distance birds fly,
they fly, but they do not sing.
The night waits in the house
safe and peaceful as candles
or carts pulled by trusty mules;
my grandfather waits in the house.
You know, the moon is just a violin
that longs to be repaired.

OUR TIME (for Iz)

Has it really gone, our time,
expired lightly
as a death at night?
Sleep enters the gate
like a refugee.
The mind's well-used bundle
knots against its own universe.
I pull my essentials
from the heap
rag by rag.
Nothing bleeds.
I fall away.
My dispossession streams
in a long avenue
past me.

These are the days, my dear,
in which we play no part;
mornings when the sun
rises without us:
years to which
we have not been invited.

FIRST WORLD   (To my father)

The days were too heavy
to pack and carry, so
I have not brought them along,
but this does not stop them
linking their arms into years.
These afternoons wait for their tribute
of freshly baked bread in a bag,
count their achievements by
the number of letters answered.
A long time is time
when the sun leans the other way,
and the colic wind howls.
I stand at the top of my shadow
in dread of its unfamiliarity
fierce and first-born.
I have found the sky from which
many things fell; a place
where the coupons make sense
and your money will really come back
if you're not satisfied. And I'm not.
I have come to the guarantor,
everything works, everything fits;
thy kingdom comes first.

                    They say
mine comes third, for the days
were too heavy to carry, so everyone
took turns, and the sun stayed
with us all the time.

                    Like memory
it kept us real, and it kept us back.

INTRODUCTION BY AN AUNT

There was something about Death
when first we met
through introduction by an aunt,
that far outlasts my fear...
a gentleness of smell
that has remained
within a place which, less defined,
is more enduring.
The collections of a life
whose sole remaining use
is their belonging
that crept along with
time's stealthy cataracts.
The neighbouring dust
that visits unceremoniously,
wordless pastors
bringing piety,
bringing peace.
The unmajestic warmth
of dying light,
a weakened phrase,
a lisp of sight.

AUTUMN

It is not till the end of autumn
that the leaves give up, that they
let go their mouthless souls, jumping
from fire through a tree's window...
it's been one helluva carnival!
Men in dark coats stand winterly
at the edge of the forest, come
to interview leaves; they just have
to wait, but like death they are good
at being inevitable. Meanwhile
the bonfire gallops through the trees
eating them like supper, and a woman
dances flamenco, brittle and dry,
with quick heels, and her gossip
is clever, cruel as fine fingers.
She wears a red rose in her hair
and the rose laughs at the bull
in her man full of Sangria. Were you
invited to autumn? That bitch is
in there, so damned beautiful that
she betrays everything! Only
the return tickets of the sun
unfurl her skirts, and the wind
lifts her thoughts, they fold as they
fall into secrets behind her. She waits
exquisitely at the moment when
the music must dance for her instead,
and the sound that you hear cannot be
the castanets, but the journey
of the leaves as they hustle home
along the road.

ONE HUNDRED YEARS (FOR GABRIEL MARQUEZ)

Old men tell better tales.
Somewhere, in exile,
between rumour
and the slow revenge of memory,
the veins of a continent
crawl like snakes between stones.

You laugh from the belly
of the tribe's womb,
on the vocabulary of vultures
words fly to carnage;
black, black Orpheus.

Before these cities
came to look the same,
truth had its own shape,
magic was magic.

And she who wandered
through the generations
was love,
collecting bones,
listening to confessions
returned upon a rosary of blood

the knowledge
and the mercy of the mind,
they are insomniac.

THE WHITE FLOWER

You gave me a white flower
with its eyes closed,
pages of white paper
without print.
It reminded me
of a Chinese ambassador.
I am afraid of this flower
for walls are white;
they say light is white
and that white is often wrong,
but my flower will open
only at night.

Night is a neighbour's room;
I can just see the door
as it closes.
We are saints without worlds
and we wait for the sun.
My white flower
stretched herself tight
like an opaque gloom,
she has no face
only one blind eye
that does not glow.
Night is a crematorium
at work in the next room,
angels of white wax,
flowers with white canes.

AFTERNOON

Play for me
one more time
Afternoon of a Faun
Debussy...
I have never seen a faun
but afternoons
have often sat with me.
I will imagine
as the music plays
a faun
is something far away
that runs beside a stream,
and when the music ends
light sits in the trees
near stream and faun
like old friends.

EVENING

I open my eyes to darkness;
the hills philosophical
are sculptures of stone,
the moon has not opened,
she's as late as she likes.
I hear a dancer in the trees,
she must be elastic and soft
and she sees in the dark
like a cat.

Out there
night stains like blood
through a veinless lake
where there is no moon.

AT NIGHT

Night leans over my shoulder
as the walls embrace.
Darkness comforts me
with the iambic
rememberings of prayers.
I stir the net of a dream,
walk a path of brail
counting each lit star
like a rosary bead
in my myopic sleep.
At the gates of life we leave
the night-watch, an insomniac owl,
the cricket who won't go home,
the moon, a rumour of the sun,
its ghostly otherness, so in the dark
the world won't lose its way.

ONLY THE MOON

Dawn breaks,
but the world is not in half.
I am here,
hung from my beginning,
fed slowly by my death.
Men wander the earth
like fingers of a tribe
circling their hand,
plundering their own dream.
Here the morning papers tell
the terror of the night we shared
when the moon
was the only light left on.

YESTERDAY

The stairs
are all folding,
and yesterday's
holding a rose.
We sit and we wait,
all-embraced
like a hedge,
and the moon all alone
strolls in through the door;
it's late
and she's holding a rose.
The gate folds its arms,
the roof rolls up its walls,
the lids of the windows shut.

The wind
with fine fingers
pulls the world away.

FRAGMENT

This small piece
of broken glass
fits nowhere
but here;
had you but known!
For when you let it go
it disappeared,
it was too small
to find again,
it had no mind to know,
nor mouth to tell you so,
that it was made
for there.

A MINUTE'S SILENCE

A minute's silence
and the second hand
walks the familiar journey.
The clock ticks but it has no heart
and the minute hand
guides time
through its final walk,
then closes the perfect circle
of a life.

MUSIC

Music
pulls its sweet thread
through me
till I am
nearer me than love or fear

Music
pulls at the last chance
of me
until I am
lovely as a leaf

a leaf
after rain.

Tearless, unending water...
the back of youth
smooth and shining

Peace lies at the edge of night
the placid moonlight of space
the effortless health of time
in God's place.

LANDSCAPE

Haven't I been here before,
at the edge of an afternoon
oiled and intricate?
The landscape takes me in.
The wind worries the knots of my belief.
Today I ask the rain

whose are the eyes
from which
such sorrow falls?

Love and death
Love and death
the layers of green in an afternoon
the impudence of a bird's flight overhead.

MEMORYECTOMY

Part by part
appears to be working so well,
and yet there's a falling apart...
no, not falling...
nor is anything
torn asunder or pulled;
rather, pruned neatly,
stripped clean of the binding
of frayed, dried leaves
that composts...
cleverly lanced scars:
a memoryectomy.

But keloids
were all little voices
that told tales in the dark
of triumphs;
ragged battle flags,
tiny In Requiems
saluting old pain,
bundled headstones
with their quotations.

Now they bloom
without the message
of scent.

VENICE

Bloom on the dark sea
lily of spite;
evil threads its webbed bridges.
A cat
walks on your tombed, still heart.
The night has no belly,
the light no kingdom.
Wicked old men
smoke behind secrets
and the city sinks,
the sparkle of glass
played by the icy wind.

I fell
through despotic thunder
past ambassadors of rain.
The shoulders of mountains
climbed above me
as I fell
through the muscles of the sun,
arched and shining
from the sky's trampoline.
I fell
to the afternoon,
flowers at tea,
a picket of arms
to surround the garden;
past the attic window
that waits for the moon.
The light faded like paint
into the sea
as I fell through Lethe,
past the hands of my friends,
beneath the faceless water
where the children float like bubbles.
I fell
through my own throat
to a wordless thunder.
The rain played no obituary
and the lightning
lifted its skirt over the water.

GOING

Folding the car
neatly up the road,
like the finalising of a matter,
I drove in safety
with a law-abiding confidence
into the starless night.
I hadn't thought, my world,
that leaving here
was such a simple thing.
A tidy usher
in a wingless coat
ticked my small name and disembodied me;
I became an entering thought
upon the void.

Who knows now where
the small, blue car is parked,
or if it drives again,
or where the patient body
I was loaned
to batter and betray
is laid to rest;
but through these endless miles
they speed,
riding my thoughts.

A FAREWELL

This is the strangest exile,
gentle friend,
no longer strange to you
winged to an endless freedom.
I know not where
that bird has flown
which yesterday was here
trespassing my morning,
but memory keeps it near.
I met you once
upon a different journey
when, like a negative reversed,
you were migrant
to the island of my heart.
It is too late to save
the iris in the grass;
blown flowers are another loveliness.
Is it the drifting song
that leaves its feathered legend
to apocrypha, your flight beyond time?
No acreage bounds the truth
of your long night,
the moon knows no anxiety.

PASSOVER

Sometimes
you are in my room
where I keep my mind
and my desk and my sanity
and all the drawers neatly occupied
with my consequences.

Sometimes you are not.

Sometimes
you turn inside out
feathered with prickly quills
of an ancient pain, borrowed
from victims of horror, their holocausts,
and you the victim of sorrow,
their sorrow.

Sometimes you are not.

Sometimes
you are here with me
prowling between our love and worth,
smoothing each other's edges
'til we almost fit;
then something passes over
and the phone shrieks
or they arrive shrill as geese
to use you up,
feed you their worry beads,
take you away.

Sometimes I give up.

FOR CAROL JACOBS

We had not thought that dreams
were hard as limestone,
fixed as the abusive face of rock;
not known time was unleavened,
a trail continuing from the past:
inevitable steps of our unselving.
We grew like words out of our fathers
that only echo at their ending.
Endurance is the quality of bone.
Friend, we are halfway there.

But we bequeath the music of a woman's beauty,
the sunlight of a journeying mind,
the comfort of our hearts, our children,
pebbles chuckling to the sea's tales.
Time seemed so green, so otherwise, at Mona;
slowly the years engrave.
All that we know is fragile now,
our grief like tender defiance
of a sea-wave's heart,
which fades with its own foam.

ON THE DEATH OF A FRIEND'S FRIEND (FOR MYRTH)

Death,
the hardest thing,
a death that now belongs to you

grief,
the loneliest station
late within the seasons of the soul
where form takes on an autumn vesting

the wind is stirring in the pines
slow tears from a distant flute,
wordless pulses spilled against
the throat's nested silence.

I offer puzzled words
dead soldiers of a sacrifice
a poem of cut flowers
gathered in a wreath

But you will walk the platform
where no train arrives

again
and then again
and this is grief

and this is death
and this is life.

THE CHILD

Awake at night the rain
plays the piano on my roof;
I hear no notes but know
the thoughts of the wind.

The night is awake, or sleeps
like a horse on its feet;
the words of the night
gallop along the breeze.

I am alone except
for the child I used to be;
I listen to the night
and the child holds onto me.

The moon is a poem in the sky
whose truth I cannot see
not because I do not understand
but because I don't believe.

Wake up stars and open
all the doors in heaven;
let my songs shine in
your avenues to the sun.

LETTER TO MY SON

Beloved Luke,
the season's brown as you left it,
for in these islands even gods remain the same.
Outside the window, over the mahogany's lap,
flounces a skirt as bright as mangoes peeled.
My aunt, your aunt,
is youthless as she always was,
and seems to pray so much these days
in that despotic way which people do
when they have memorised the lines for years
and hurl them like cross stones at birds
who try to fly away.
I visited your beach the other day
and looked for shells at the sea's rim
to save for you, some singing
the ocean's hymn at the core,
and do you know, my love,
the waves remembered you, lurching at me
and wagging their wet puppy-tails of spray
as they tossed and turned to see
if you had come along. Next year, I said....

the sea will be the same
but you will be
an inch nearer to me
in our photographs

Brother Drum has lost his dog
who bore the solemn name of "Psalms"
like a suit too big for him;
we watched him commit himself to death
with that heart-breaking discipline,

43

the gift of simple life,
which knows the futility of challenge
and is at peace with the design.

I miss you,
Mum.

BOB MARLEY'S DEAD (FOR DRUM)

The moon is full
heavy yellow
Marley's dead
and there is prophecy

Hallelujah
Jah is singing on the moon
and all our pain
is like the shadow of a branch
across its face;
it's not the King who lives
long live the King
it is the Kingdom lives

My island is a mother
burying wombs
I rise, at my beginning
the squalor
the flower

The moon is dread
she bleeds
Marley's dead
and there is prophecy

The Kingdom lives
a heart of drums
a small town throbs,
we have begun
the phoenix
from a mulch of bones

I rise beyond
a fantasy
I wake
I break faith
with the white dream

The moon is black
my mother sings with me
Oh Marley's dead
and there is prophecy.

GALLOPING WILD

I must gallop wild as the lawless night
I must have freedom and time to chase the moon
to remember the bite of a branch in the wind
that language that is all of vowels;
I must burn darkly without fire
where my owl is an ancient whore
and these letters are the fists of the dark
and death is the edge of the mountain.
There are many devils in me
and my mind is the will of my dream
the stars as they spit and spark
cannot wake me.

CROPOVER

Now they have cut the canes
and I don't know whether they leave
like Jews hoarded off to Treblinka,
or protesting children
to Sunday school,
but the land is gross and torn
and I am afflicted.

DROUGHT

I shake the air
and it is empty,
falling away in my hands
like dead hairs.
The smooth skull
rocks and chuckles
in the afternoon
long past conscience or grief
or rain.
Someone carved a name
when the tree had sap,
its letters now keloid scars
over dead memory.
Drought strips
the tree's roof
and love's heart.
I cannot remember
the Lord's Prayer
nor my seven times table,
cannot turn down the wind,
and the doors of my eyes
cannot shut.

I will wax
the afternoon's skull,
plait what's left
of the sky's hair,
for the funeral.

THE SEA TODAY

There's something desperate
about the sea today,
who had withdrawn for many months
in long remorse,
swallowing her pain
in slow, sulking gulps;
had held her tongue,
sat upon the things she knows
like a thick paperweight;
and when I moved at night
she sloshed around my dream
as though she lay
hot-water-bottled next to me.

But not today.
She is the angry sister of the moon
and leaves her tears
shining on the shore's lids,
wringing her waves
like laundry on the rocks.
For all her wetness
she is hard and salt
and I am thirsty
hearing her wounds
bleed along the coast.

RARON

A poem in memory of
Rainer Maria Rilke
Dedicated to David Boxer

"Rose, oh pure contradiction, joy
of being no one's sleep under so many lids."

Rainer Maria Rilke

Where a man is buried, life knots
his time on earth. How easily we pass
another's world and journey on.
Rilke knew that first he had to reach Raron.
An ancient supplication hurled against
the sky, a mountain unarranged, urged
by the subterranean murmur of its soul.
In nature it is only man who interrupts
the landscape time has harmonised.
Four large bells in a denture's grin
to smash the gentleness a Sunday brings,
its library of thoughts, searchings
through shelves, each precious ownness of mind
drifting down its meditation. Bells
like Cyclopean eyes burst through
the brow of ground, they break
the careful scaffolding of silence, they shake
the magic balance of spirit and self
sensing each other in the space they share.
Grief plants its obedient row of pines,
its story faithfully sewn,
as safely as the sea's within a shell,
in the parable of a cone:
each keeps a promise at Raron.

Is it only the old who climb this mountain
pacing their weakened steps up the quiet path?
Each gloved hand finds its pocket,
not to intrude upon an earth no longer theirs.
Why do they search the ground as they climb,
piercing the air like unicorns,
with their minds instead of their eyes?
What do they find, who move the road
out of their way 'til they reach the gate?
They do not see the houses on either side
vining the path like conscience,
nor do the houses see them, shuttered
against time. But they survive the centuries
in their staggered trek, sharing no sorrow
with the old who use their last time, spend
their small breath, what's left to them to spend.
Is there a window through which they pass,
escaping souls? Behind them closes a road.
The mountain's blood babbles through time
at the watering hole. Before the box
was strapped, flowing through the wait
in the waiting room, in and out of memory,
and souls, and stations; flowing after
other worlds are reached and left,
mountain without end: no effort
hones eternity. That man must die,
and knows it, enobles him.

RARON III

Pass through the gate, it neither opens
nor shuts; only the body folds
its curtains behind. Consider the rose
who begins her journey closed.
Come to the lawn of beds, each resting
brave tucked into the sum of his worth.
A host of crosses turns at the sound of steps
their arms outstretched like mendicants
beseeching memory for each one's
mute constituent. They mark the place
where man's imagination left its luggage
as it journeyed on. Beyond, the Alps
sleep through their fame, commanding
the horizon, an athlete in repose
whose baton passed to legend;
which shift so imperceptibly, our lives
pass as a bird's flight. Earth's misty breath
mutters in prayer over the valley.
As I reached the mountained church,
incidental as a station stop,
waiting to meet Rilke, I knew
that man's imagination travels on.

Smell too wears clothes;
beneath the manners of a rose
a heart more scarlet than its skin
unwraps its clichés of memory.
The mysterious mother
on which you lie, coddled
by the mountain's hip,
was the souvenir you took from home,
once an oasis tender
by the distance that it kept.
This is life's winter,
time of the trees' repose
shed of their thoughts.
You, who are no one's sleep
in savouring, let us honour you.
Thorns cannot stop this wind
that struggles past us
to applaud the Alps.
To hold the ghost of a rose
is nature's gift of eternity.

Born in Cornwall, England of an English mother and a Jamaican father, Rachel Manley came to Jamaica at the age of two. She grew up with her grandparents, N.W. Manley, intellectual shaper and leader of Jamaica's nationalist movement, and Edna Manley, the sculptor and energetic promoter of Jamaican arts. Her father, a trade unionist and politician, she was involved in a life which was 'tumultuous and inspiring — rooted in the spirit of Jamaica'.

She is the author of two previous collections of poetry, *Prisms* and *Poems 2* and the editor of *Edna Manley: The Diaries*.

She has two sons.